SCHOLASTIC

READ & RESPOND

Bringing the best books to life in the classroom

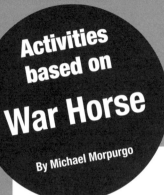

Activities based on

War Horse

By Michael Morpurgo

Terms and conditions

IMPORTANT – PERMITTED USE AND WARNINGS – READ CAREFULLY BEFORE USING

Copyright in the software contained in this CD-ROM and in its accompanying material belongs to Scholastic Limited. All rights reserved. © 2016 Scholastic Ltd.

Save for these purposes, or as expressly authorised in the accompanying materials, the software may not be copied, reproduced, used, sold, licensed, transferred, exchanged, hired, or exported in whole or in part or in any manner or form without the prior written consent of Scholastic Ltd. Any such unauthorised use or activities are prohibited and may give rise to civil liabilities and criminal prosecutions.

The material contained on this CD-ROM may only be used in the context for which it was intended in *Read & Respond,* and is for use only by the purchaser or purchasing institution that has purchased the book and CD-ROM. Permission to download images is given for purchasers only and not for users from any lending service. Any further use of the material contravenes Scholastic Ltd's copyright and that of other rights holders.

This CD-ROM has been tested for viruses at all stages of its production. However, we recommend that you run virus-checking software on your computer systems at all times. Scholastic Ltd cannot accept any responsibility for any loss, disruption or damage to your data or your computer system that may occur as a result of using either the CD-ROM or the data held on it.

IF YOU ACCEPT THE ABOVE CONDITIONS YOU MAY PROCEED TO USE THE CD-ROM.

Recommended system requirements:
Windows: XP (Service Pack 3), Vista (Service Pack 2), Windows 7 or Windows 8 with 2.33GHz processor
Mac: OS 10.6 to 10.8 with Intel Core™ Duo processor
1GB RAM (recommended)
1024 x 768 Screen resolution
CD-ROM drive (24x speed recommended)
Adobe Reader (version 9 recommended for Mac users)
Broadband internet connections (for installation and updates)

For all technical support queries (including no CD drive), please phone Scholastic Customer Services on 0845 6039091.

Designed using Adobe Indesign
Scholastic Education, an imprint of Scholastic Ltd
Book End, Range Road, Witney, Oxfordshire, OX29 0YD
Registered office: Westfield Road, Southam, Warwickshire CV47 0RA

Printed and bound by Ashford Colour Press
© 2016 Scholastic Ltd
1 2 3 4 5 6 7 8 9 6 7 8 9 0 1 2 3 4 5

British Library Cataloguing-in-Publication Data
A catalogue record for this book is available from the British Library.
ISBN 978-1407-16063-4

Due to the nature of the web, we cannot guarantee the content or links of any site mentioned. We strongly recommend that teachers check websites before using them in the classroom.

Author Pam Dowson
Editorial team Rachel Morgan, Jenny Wilcox, Sarah Sodhi and Jennie Clifford
Series designer Neil Salt
Designer Alice Duggan
Illustrator Ray and Corinne Burrows/Beehive Illustration
Digital development Hannah Barnett, Phil Crothers and MWA Technologies Private Ltd

Acknowledgements
The publishers gratefully acknowledge permission to reproduce the following copyright material:
Egmont UK Limited for the use of the extract from *War Horse* by Michael Morpurgo. Text copyright © 1982 Michael Morpurgo. Cover illustration copyright © 2006 from the poster for the National Theatre's stage adaptation of *War Horse*, first staged October 2007. Published by Egmont UK Limited and used with permission.

Every effort has been made to trace copyright holders for the works reproduced in this book, and the publishers apologise for any inadvertent omissions.

CONTENTS ▼

INTRODUCTION

Read & Respond provides teaching ideas related to a specific children's book. The series focuses on best-loved books and brings you ways to use them to engage your class and enthuse them about reading.

The book is divided into different sections:

- **About the book and author:** gives you some background information about the book and the author.

- **Guided reading:** breaks the book down into sections and gives notes for using it with guided reading groups. A bookmark has been provided on page 12 containing comprehension questions. The children can be directed to refer to these as they read.

- **Shared reading:** provides extracts from the children's book with associated notes for focused work. There is also one non-fiction extract that relates to the children's book.

- **Grammar, punctuation & spelling:** provides word-level work related to the children's book so you can teach grammar, punctuation and spelling in context.

- **Plot, character & setting:** contains activity ideas focused on the plot, characters and the setting of the story.

- **Talk about it:** has speaking and listening activities related to the children's book. These activities may be based directly on the children's book or be broadly based on the themes and concepts of the story.

- **Get writing:** provides writing activities related to the children's book. These activities may be based directly on the children's book or be broadly based on the themes and concepts of the story.

- **Assessment:** contains short activities that will help you assess whether the children have understood concepts and curriculum objectives. They are designed to be informal activities to feed into your planning.

The activities follow the same format:

- **Objective:** the objective for the lesson. It will be based upon a curriculum objective, but will often be more specific to the focus being covered.

- **What you need:** a list of resources you need to teach the lesson, including digital resources (printable pages, interactive activities and media resources, see page 5).

- **What to do:** the activity notes.

- **Differentiation:** this is provided where specific and useful differentiation advice can be given to support and/or extend the learning in the activity. Differentiation by providing additional adult support has not been included as this will be at a teacher's discretion based upon specific children's needs and ability, as well as the availability of support.

The activities are numbered for reference within each section and should move through the text sequentially – so you can use the lesson while you are reading the book. Once you have read the book, most of the activities can be used in any order you wish.

Below are brief guidance notes for using the CD-ROM. For more detailed information, please click on the '?' button in the top right-hand corner of the screen.

The program contains the following:
- the extract pages from the book
- all of the photocopiable pages from the book
- additional printable pages
- interactive on-screen activities
- media resources.

Getting started

Put the CD-ROM into your CD-ROM drive. If you do not have a CD-ROM drive, phone Scholastic Customer Services on 0845 6039091.

- For Windows users, the install wizard should autorun. If it fails to do so, then navigate to your CD-ROM drive and follow the installation process.
- For Mac users, copy the disk image file to your hard drive. After it has finished copying, double click it to mount the disk image. Navigate to the mounted disk image and run the installer. After installation, the disk image can be unmounted and the DMG can be deleted from the hard drive.
- To install on a network, see the ReadMe file located on the CD-ROM (navigate to your drive).

To complete the installation of the program you need to open the program and click 'Update' in the pop-up. Please note – this CD-ROM is web-enabled and the content will be downloaded from the internet to your hard drive to populate the CD-ROM with the relevant resources. This only needs to be done on first use. After this you will be able to use the CD-ROM without an internet connection. If at any point any content is updated, you will receive another pop-up upon start up when there is an internet connection.

Main menu

The Main menu is the first screen that appears. Here you can access: terms and conditions, registration links, how to use the CD-ROM and credits. To access a specific book, click on the relevant button (only titles installed will be available). You can filter by the

drop-down lists if you wish. You can search all resources by clicking 'Search' in the bottom left-hand corner. You can also log in and access favourites that you have bookmarked.

Resources

By clicking on a book on the Main menu, you are taken to the resources for that title. The resources are: Media, Interactives, Extracts and Printables. Select the category and then launch a resource by clicking the play button.

Teacher settings

In the top right-hand corner of the screen is a small 'T' icon. This is the teacher settings area. It is password protected. The password is: login. This area will allow you to choose the print quality settings for interactive activities ('Default' or 'Best') and also allow you to check for updates to the program or re-download all content to the disk via 'Refresh all content'. You can also set up user logins so that you can save and access favourites. Once a user is set up, they can enter by clicking the login link underneath the 'T' and '?' buttons.

Search

You can access an all resources search by clicking the search button on the bottom left of the Main menu. You can search for activities by type (using the drop-down filter) or by keyword by typing into the box. You can then assign resources to your favourites area or launch them directly from the search area.

CURRICULUM LINKS

Section	Activity	Curriculum objectives
Guided reading		Comprehension: To check that the book makes sense to them, discussing their understanding and exploring the meaning of words in context. To draw inferences such as inferring characters' feelings, thoughts and motives from their actions, and justifying inferences with evidence. To identify how language, structure and presentation contribute to meaning.
Shared reading	1	Comprehension: To check that the book makes sense to them, discussing their understanding and exploring the meaning of words in context.
	2	Comprehension: To draw inferences such as inferring characters' feelings, thoughts and motives from their actions, and justifying inferences with evidence.
	3	Comprehension: To discuss and evaluate how authors use language, including figurative language, considering the impact on the reader.
	4	Comprehension: To retrieve, record and present information from non-fiction.
Grammar, punctuation & spelling	1	Composition: To use modal verbs or adverbs to indicate degrees of possibility.
	2	Composition: To use a range of devices to build cohesion within and across paragraphs.
	3	Composition: To use brackets, dashes or commas to indicate parenthesis.
	4	Composition: To use a colon to introduce a list and use semi-colons within lists.
	5	Transcription: To spell words ending in 'able', 'ible', 'ably' and 'ibly'.
	6	Transcription: To spell words containing the letter string 'ough'.
Plot, character & setting	1	Comprehension: To summarise the main ideas drawn from more than one paragraph, identifying key details that support the main ideas.
	2	Comprehension: To draw inferences such as inferring characters' feelings, thoughts and motives from their actions, and justifying with evidence.
	3	Comprehension: To identify how language contributes to meaning.
	4	Comprehension: To summarise the main ideas drawn from more than one paragraph, identifying key details that support the main ideas.
	5	Comprehension: To identify and discuss themes in and across a wide range of writing.
	6	Comprehension: To identify how structure contributes to meaning.
	7	Comprehension: To discuss and evaluate how authors use language, considering the impact on the reader.
	8	Comprehension: To draw inferences, such as inferring characters' feelings, thoughts and motives from their actions, and justifying with evidence.

Section	Activity	Curriculum objectives
Talk about it	1	Spoken language: To participate in role play and improvisation.
	2	Spoken language: To participate in role play and improvisation.
	3	Spoken language: To ask relevant questions to extend their understanding and knowledge.
	4	Spoken language: To participate in role play and improvisation.
	5	Spoken language: To maintain attention and participate actively in collaborative conversations, staying on topic and initiating and responding to comments.
	6	Spoken language: To give well-structured descriptions, explanations and narratives for different purposes, including for expressing feelings.
Get writing	1	Composition: To select appropriate grammar and vocabulary, understanding how such choices can change and enhance meaning.
	2	Composition: To describe settings, characters and atmosphere in narratives, and integrate dialogue to convey character and advance the action.
	3	Composition: To use further organisational and presentational devices to structure text and to guide the reader (for example, headings, bullet points, underlining).
	4	Composition: To describe settings, characters and atmosphere in narratives, and integrate dialogue to convey character and advance the action.
	5	Composition: To précis longer passages.
	6	Composition: To describe settings, characters and atmosphere in narratives, and integrate dialogue to convey character and advance the action.
Assessment	1	Comprehension: To recommend books that they have read to their peers, giving reasons for their choices.
	2	Composition: To describe settings, characters and atmosphere in narratives and integrate dialogue to convey character and advance the action.
	3	Transcription: To spell words ending with 'able', 'ible', 'ably' and 'ibly'.
	4	Composition: To use modal verbs or adverbs to indicate degrees of possibility.
	5	Comprehension: To ask questions to improve their understanding.
	6	Composition: To describe settings, characters and atmosphere in narratives and integrate dialogue to convey character and advance the action.

WAR HORSE

About the book

War Horse tells the gripping and traumatic personal story of Joey, one of the many horses requisitioned by the British Army at the outbreak of World War I. Written in the first person, we see Joey's life through his eyes, from being separated from his mother at auction to being befriended and trained by Albert on the family farm. Albert is heartbroken when Joey is taken to war, and vows to join up when he is old enough to travel to France to find his beloved horse. Joey's story is one of both love and despair. He is fortunate in his association with Topthorn, a horse who acts as mentor and friend, and by a succession of owners, including Captain Nicholls, who first requisitioned him, Emilie, a little French girl on whose farm he is billeted, and Friedrich, a German soldier who cares for him when he is captured by the enemy. But he suffers dreadful hardship on the muddy battlefields of northern France, loses friends and, eventually, running scared from the roar of battle, finds himself trapped in the barbed wire of no man's land. An English and a German soldier free him and he is taken to a British veterinary hospital where, amazingly, he is reunited with Albert, who nurses him back to health. Morpurgo is known as a master storyteller and *War Horse* is a fine example of his craft. The book was made into a successful film in 2011.

About the author

Michael Morpurgo was born in St Albans, Hertfordshire in 1943. He studied English and French before becoming a primary school teacher. His experience of reading stories to the children in his class first made him think of becoming a writer. 'There was a magic in it for me,' he said when explaining what first drew him to writing. He has written over a hundred books, preferring to write by hand rather than use a computer. In 1976 he and his wife set up Farms for City Children, a charity that helps inner-city children experience life in the country. He spends a lot of his time working on one of the three farms near his home in Devon. Michael Morpurgo has won many awards, both in the UK and in France. He has been shortlisted for the Carnegie Medal four times and was Children's Laureate from 2003 to 2005. He has honorary doctorates from a number of universities and is president of the Book Trust. He was awarded the OBE for services to literature in 2006. He has three children and six grandchildren.

Key facts
War Horse
Author: Michael Morpurgo
First published: 1982
Awards: Runner-up for the Whitbread Award 1982
Did you know?: *War Horse* has been translated into 43 languages. A stage play adaptation was made in 2007 and has been performed in London's West End and on Broadway in New York. A film version was made in 2011 and a radio play in 2008.

Early days

Ask the children if they know of the book or film. If not, ask: *What does the cover suggest the book is about?* Ask them to read the 'Author's note' to themselves. Do they know the significance of the date, 1914? Ask: *What does this date suggest to you?* They may guess that the story is based on fact – something they can check later online. Ask them to read the first two paragraphs of Chapter 1, noting that it is written in the first person, in the voice of a horse. As they read the rest of Chapter 1, ask them to consider question 8 on the Guided Reading bookmark (page 12) about language use, discussing their observations.

Continue reading to Chapter 2, focusing on question 1 on the bookmark, about Joey's feelings as Albert trains him. Ask the children to give evidence to support their views. Ask the children to find examples of where the author has shown, rather than told, us about the attitudes of different characters here (for example, Albert's mother's comments about the outbreak of war).

Ask the children to read Chapter 3 for the next session, considering question 11 on the bookmark.

A new life

Begin by discussing the children's thoughts about Albert's father from question 11 on the Guided Reading bookmark. Was Albert's mother justified in her defence of her husband?

Move on to read Chapter 4, where Joey is sold to the army. This is Joey's third owner and marks another change of role. Suggest that, as they read the book, the children keep a timeline of the changes of owner and role Joey encounters throughout his life.

As they read Chapter 4, ask the children to focus on question 1 on the bookmark, discussing their

ideas about Joey's feelings. Do they think he would understand what was happening? Does their opinion of Albert's father change by the end of the chapter, when he explains why he has to sell Joey?

Continue with Chapter 5, where Joey is trained as a cavalry horse. Ask the children to consider question 2 on the bookmark, about Captain Nicholls' feelings towards Joey. How do his comments affect the way Corporal Perkins cares for Joey? Do they spot the link in this chapter to the painting referred to in the 'Author's note'?

Ask the children to read Chapter 6 in preparation for the next session.

Into war

Ask the children to describe Joey's experiences of his Channel crossing and first battle in Chapter 6. What would his emotions be at finding a friend in Topthorn and losing Captain Nicholls?

Move on to Chapter 7. Do the children know the word 'reveille' in the opening sentence? Ask them to consider question 7 on the Guided Reading bookmark as they read, discussing their thoughts about humans confiding in Joey.

After reading the letter from Trooper Warren's mother, ask: *How would receiving this letter affect him?*

As they read to the end of the chapter, ask the children to note words and phrases that are particularly effective in portraying the journey to the battlefield. Discuss their choices, asking them to explain their selection.

Continue with Chapter 8, focusing on question 9 on the bookmark, noting language used to describe the battle. In this chapter, Joey sees death and destruction all around him, including the shooting of injured horses. He is captured by the enemy and is separated from the two men who have cared for him. How do the events in the chapter make the children feel? How does this reflect on Michael Morpurgo's writing?

In preparation for the next session, ask the children to read Chapters 9 and 10, focusing on question 12 on the bookmark.

Captured!

Begin by asking the children to share their observations on Chapters 9 and 10, with reference to question 12 on the Guided Reading bookmark. Did they see more similarities or differences between the German and British perspectives? Ask: *What reasons do you think Michael Morpurgo had for including this series of events?* (For example, he may have wanted readers to see the futility of war or it may have simply added to the tension of the story.)

Move on to Chapter 11, reading the first paragraph. Refer the children to question 6 on the bookmark, about the passing of time, discussing their responses and looking back at earlier chapters for comparison. (The story covers many years, this is a useful way to show time passing.)

Reading on, look at the section in Chapter 11 starting 'The hay was almost gathered in…' to '…too tired to reply' in the following paragraph. Point out that there is no attempt to anthropomorphise the horses – the author has not tried to give them human voices. Why do the children think this decision was made?

As they continue reading Chapters 11 and 12, ask the children to focus on question 3 on the bookmark, comparing Joey's feelings about the events described. From being happy working on the farm with Emilie and her grandfather, Joey and Topthorn are taken back to the front line, suffering dreadfully. Pause from time to time to allow the children to talk about their reactions to the conditions experienced by the horses.

As you read the final part of Chapter 12, beginning 'I first noticed', talk about the bond between Joey and Topthorn, and how Joey would feel seeing his friend failing.

Ask the children to read Chapters 13 and 14 before the next session, focusing on question 4 on the bookmark.

No man's land

Ask what evidence the children found in Chapter 14 for the bond between Joey and Topthorn. Move on to Chapter 15, where Joey runs to escape the tanks and ends up trapped in no man's land. This is a powerful description of terrifying events, which some children may find upsetting, so be prepared to pause for discussion at any point. Talk about the poignancy of Joey finally being driven to leave Topthorn and the opening sentence of paragraph 3, noting the significance of the arrival of tanks, underlining the previous need for horses, which they will replace.

As they read on, ask the children to note any places where the description particularly affected them, explaining why. Focus on the dialogue beginning 'There it is again, Sarge'. Ask: *What nationality are the soldiers?* (British) *How can we tell?* (Their language use; the reference to Germans.) At the end of the chapter, refer to question 10 on the bookmark, about why the author chose to use the first person, discussing the children's thoughts.

Move on to Chapter 16. Do they know the significance of the white flag being flown in the second paragraph? As they read about the German and British soldiers working together to free Joey, ask them to consider again the similarities – both are prepared to suspend fighting to free the injured horse; both agree on the futility of war.

After reading about the coin toss, how do the children think Joey would feel about being 'won' by the British? Can they predict what will happen to him?

Ask them to read Chapters 17 and 18 before the next session, considering question 13 on the bookmark.

Peace at last?

Revisit Chapter 17, asking for the children's responses to question 13 on the Guided Reading bookmark, about Joey and Albert being reunited. What were their reactions to Joey's illness in Chapter 18?

Continue to Chapter 19, reading to the end of paragraph 2. It is now the summer of 1918 and we know that the war will soon end, but those involved didn't. Can the children imagine how it would feel to the soldiers?

Read on to 'here to see it'. Refer again to question 7 on the bookmark, about characters talking to Joey. Point out that this device allows us to see events from points of view other than Joey's, giving an insight into their character.

As they read to the end of the chapter, ask the children to focus on question 5 on the bookmark, about the prospects for the horses after the war has ended. Do they work out that many are likely to be sold for meat? What are their feelings about this?

In preparation for the next session, ask the children to read Chapter 20, focusing on the atmosphere evoked at the horse auction.

Home

Begin by asking the children about Chapter 20. Invite them to share sections that they felt created atmosphere particularly well, explaining their selections. Were they surprised when Emilie's grandfather bought Joey? What do they think will happen to him next?

Read the first paragraph of the final chapter. Ask: *Whose feelings are being described here?* (Sgt Thunder, Major Martin, Albert, an unnamed soldier.)

Have the children noticed that Joey's feelings are rarely described, only descriptions of what happened to him? He talks about his physical feelings but only briefly about his emotional ones. Nevertheless, have they been able to work out what Joey's feelings might be? How might he be feeling now?

Read on to 'Must do, mustn't it?' Do they understand the exchange between the Major and Sergeant? (They both know they arranged to bid for Joey.)

Continue reading up to 'I promised my Emilie'. Point out that now Albert knows some of what happened to Joey during the war. Ask: *How might he feel about Joey's experiences?*

Read on to 'I shall treasure it always'. Ask: *What do his actions tell us about the character of Emilie's grandfather?*

Read on to the end of the book. Do the children feel satisfied with the ending? Do they notice the humour in the final sentence? Would they recommend the book to others to read? What would their reasons be?

SCHOLASTIC
READ & RESPOND
Bringing the best books to life in the classroom

War Horse
by Michael Morpurgo

SCHOLASTIC
READ & RESPOND
Bringing the best books to life in the classroom

War Horse
by Michael Morpurgo

Focus on...
Meaning

1. How would you describe Joey's feelings during Chapters 2 and 4? Find evidence to support your views.

2. In Chapter 5, find examples to show how Captain Nicholls feels about Joey. Explain your choices.

3. Compare Joey's feelings in Chapters 11 and 12. How do circumstances affect him?

4. What evidence in Chapter 14 shows the bond between Joey and Topthorn?

5. At the horse auction in Chapter 19, the soldiers seem to know what is in store for some of the horses. What might it be?

Focus on...
Organisation

6. Many of the chapters open with a reference to time passing. Why is this a useful device in this story?

7. There are many examples of people talking to Joey as though he was human. Why do you think the author has used this device?

Focus on...
Language and features

8. In Chapter 1, note how language is used to heighten the difference between the good and bad treatment of Joey. How does this affect the pace?

9. In Chapter 8, find examples to show how language is used to describe the battle. Which words and phrases are most effective and why?

10. Why do you think the author chose to tell the story in the first person?

Focus on...
Purpose, viewpoints and effects

11. In Chapter 3, consider the character of Albert's father, and his mother's attitude towards him. Is she justified in her explanation and opinion?

12. In Chapter 9, we see the war from the German perspective. How is this different or similar to the British viewpoint?

13. How does the author build the tension when Joey and Albert are reunited in Chapter 17?

Extract 1

- Display this extract. Ask the children to read the first paragraph silently to themselves, then ask: *Which word tells us the narrator is a horse?* ('neigh') Without that word, could the rest of the paragraph describe a person's behaviour?

- Underline the word 'unconsolable', explaining that the usual spelling is 'inconsolable' but Michael Morpurgo has chosen a different prefix here.

- Read paragraph 2 and underline 'exertion'. If the children don't know it, can they work out the meaning from the context? Point out that the author has contrasted action, and implied noise, with stillness and quiet. Ask: *How does this contribute to atmosphere?*

- Read paragraph 3 and invite a volunteer to come up and highlight all the personal pronouns (there are many). Ask the children who is talking and about whom. (Albert about his father, Joey, Captain Nicholls and himself.)

- Read the final paragraph. Ask the children to identify the clauses in the first sentence, highlighting each in a different colour (there are three – the main clause and two subordinate clauses). Can they identify each subject and verb? ('soldier' and 'said'; 'cap' and 'taking'; 'brow' and 'wiping')

- Can the children suggest why Captain Nicholls thinks Albert has 'the right spirit for a soldier'? (His speech about Joey and enlisting.)

- Thinking about the whole extract, ask the children to suggest the emotions that both Joey and Albert felt during this short incident, giving evidence to support their choices.

Extract 2

- Display extract 2, showing only paragraph 1. Ask the children to read it silently and ask: *Who do you think the Corporal is saluting?* (It appears to be Joey.) What about the reference to sketching?

- Reveal the next paragraph for the children to read, where the addressee is found to be Captain Nicholls. Do they think Joey would have thought the Corporal was saluting him?

- Highlight 'Is he not the finest mount' pointing out the sentence construction, which is suggestive of the period and Captain Nicholls' class – this is not the speech of a working-class man.

- Reveal the rest of the extract for the children to read. Ask: *What are the differences between the two men's attitudes and feelings towards Joey?*

- Underline the sentence beginning 'Even his voice', asking what this description tells us about the character of the Corporal.

- Point out that most of the extract is dialogue, circling all the punctuation in paragraph 3. Note particularly the use of commas, especially before the word 'sir'. Ask the children to identify similar uses in the rest of the extract (for example, before 'Corporal'), circling their observations. This is a more complex use of the comma.

- Invite the children to work in pairs, reading the dialogue in role, taking note of the characterisation. Do they notice that the Corporal has the most to say? Is this what they would expect? Ask volunteers to perform their dialogue to the class.

Extract 3

- Display paragraph 1. Invite the children to read it to themselves then ask for their observations. Do they notice the difference in sentence length, the pace and the atmosphere? Underline the verbs, noting their variety. Discuss deliberate vocabulary choice to enhance writing.

- Reveal the rest of the extract. Highlight the fronted adverbial in the second sentence of paragraph 2. Point out the unusual construction of the sentence starting 'Better therefore'. Ask the children's opinions about the atmosphere created in this paragraph.

- Ask the children to read the remainder of the text. Invite them to highlight and share what they feel are the most effective vocabulary choices. Ask them to justify their selections. Highlight the phrase 'the fields lost their grass'. Ask: *How else might this have been expressed? Why is this choice effective?*

- Looking at the whole extract, invite the children to identify where Michael Morpurgo has used any of the five senses in his description of the events, highlighting their choices. (Mostly sight and sound, though there are allusions to touch, for example, 'lush, wet meadow'; 'sapped the strength from my legs'; 'barbed wire that first snagged and then trapped my foreleg'.)

- Invite the children to identify examples of movement in the extract, and the associated verbs, underling their choices.

- Read the final short paragraph and ask the children to suggest what might happen next.

Extract 4

- Display this extract. Ask the children to read paragraph 1 to themselves. Underline any words they identify as new to them (for example, 'spheres', 'internal combustion engine', 'equine stock', 'requisitioned'). Ask them to work out the meaning of these words from the text. Does it surprise them that horses were so important? In what ways do they think life became more difficult in Britain after the horses were requisitioned? (For example, farm work, delivering supplies, transport in general.)

- After reading paragraph 2, ask the children where horses were used by the military, highlighting their choices. Did they realise the war was fought in these countries? What is their opinion of horses being shipped from America, including wild horses? Can they suggest what conditions might have been like for the animals when crossing the Atlantic?

- After reading the rest of the extract, ask the children to identify the roles played by horses in the war, highlighting their selections. Underline the words 'cavalry', 'potential', 'plight' and 'endure'. Invite the children to work out their meanings from the text.

- Ask: *What do you think the soldiers felt about their role with the horses?* Invite them to give reasons for their opinions. The extract focuses on the horses, but can they work out what conditions would have been like for the soldiers and how this might have affected them?

- Show the children the media resource 'Horses in battle' for them to see the reality.

Extract 1

Chapter 4

It was then that I fully realised I was being abandoned and I began to neigh, a high-pitched cry of pain and anxiety that shrieked out through the village. Even old Zoey, obedient and placid as she always was, stopped and would not be moved on no matter how hard Albert's father pulled her. She turned, tossed up her head and shouted her farewell. But her cries became weaker and she was finally dragged away and out of my sight. Kind hands tried to contain me and to console me, but I was unconsolable.

I had just about given up all hope, when I saw my Albert running up towards me through the crowd, his face red with exertion. The band had stopped playing and the entire village looked on as he came up to me and put his arms around my neck.

'He's sold him, hasn't he?' he said quietly, looking up at Captain Nicholls who was holding me. 'Joey is my horse. He's my horse and he always will be, no matter who buys him. I can't stop my father from selling him, but if Joey goes with you, I go. I want to join up and stay with him.'

'You've the right spirit for a soldier, young man,' said the officer, taking off his peaked cap and wiping his brow with the back of his hand. He had black curly hair and a kind, open look on his face. 'You've the right spirit but you haven't the years. You're too young and you know it. Seventeen's the youngest we take. Come back in a year or so and then we'll see.'

Extract 2

Chapter 5

A door banged across the yard and I heard the familiar sound of boots, crisp on the cobbles. It was Corporal Samuel Perkins passing along the lines of stables on his evening rounds, stopping at each one to check until at last he came to mine. 'Good evening, sir,' he said, saluting smartly. 'Sketching again?'

'Doing my best, Corporal,' said Captain Nicholls. 'Doing my best to do him justice. Is he not the finest mount in the entire squadron? I've never seen a horse so well put together as he is, have you?'

'Oh he's special enough to look at, sir,' said the Corporal of Horse. Even his voice put my ears back, there was a thin, acid tone to it that I dreaded. 'I grant you that, but looks aren't everything, are they, sir? There's always more to a horse than meets the eye, isn't that right, sir? How shall I put it, sir?'

'However you like, Corporal,' said Captain Nicholls somewhat frostily, 'but be careful what you say for that's my horse you're speaking about, so take care.'

'Let's say I feel he has a mind of his own. Yes, let's put it that way. He's good enough out on manoeuvres – a real stayer, one of the very best – but inside the school, sir, he's a devil, and a strong devil too. Never been properly schooled, sir, you can tell that. Farm-horse he is and farm trained. If he's to make a cavalry horse, sir, he'll have to learn to accept the disciplines. He has to learn to obey instantly and instinctively. You don't want a prima donna under you while the bullets start flying.'

Extract 3

Chapter 15

I ran I knew not where. I ran till I could no longer hear that dreadful rattle and until the guns seemed far away. I remember crossing a river again, galloping through empty farmyards, jumping fences and ditches and abandoned trenches, and clattering through deserted, ruined villages before I found myself grazing that evening in a lush, wet meadow and drinking from a clear, pebbly brook. And then exhaustion finally overtook me, sapped the strength from my legs and forced me to lie down and sleep.

When I woke it was dark and the guns were firing once more all around me. No matter where I looked it seemed, the sky was lit with the yellow flashes of gunfire and intermittent white glowing lights that pained my eyes and showered daylight briefly on to the countryside around me. Whichever way I went it seemed it had to be towards the guns. Better therefore I thought to stay where I was. Here at least I had grass in plenty and water to drink.

I had made up my mind to do just that when there was an explosion of white light above my head and the rattle of a machine-gun split the night air, the bullets whipping into the ground beside me. I ran again and kept running into the night, stumbling frequently in the ditches and hedges until the fields lost their grass and the trees were mere stumps against the flashing skyline. Wherever I went now there were great craters in the ground filled with murky, stagnant water.

It was as I staggered out of one such crater that I lumbered into an invisible coil of barbed wire that first snagged then trapped my foreleg.

Extract 4

Horses in World War I

Before the outbreak of war in 1914, the British Army already had 250,000 horses. Although this may seem unusual to us today, horses were still widely used in all spheres of life, as the internal combustion engine was in its infancy. With the prospect of war in Europe, it was therefore vital to increase the army's equine stock, so many thousands of animals were requisitioned for war use, making life difficult for those left at home.

While most horses were used on the battlefields of northern France, some served in the Balkans, the Middle East, Egypt and Italy. Over the course of the war, Britain used over a million horses, replenishing stocks with weekly deliveries from America, a thousand at a time, some of them wild.

Both horses and mules were used – the majority for hauling supplies, medicines and wounded soldiers – many were ridden, while others pulled gun carriages and more than 75,000 were cavalry horses, fighting on the front line. Many soldiers did their best to care for the horses (after all, they were vital to potential success) and there were veterinary hospitals, but often conditions overcame the best of intentions. After months and years of conflict, some men became hardened to the horses' plight and had not the energy or will to look after them properly. As the war progressed, conditions worsened, with rations in short supply and battlegrounds becoming mud-clogged. Often there was no shelter. As well as hunger, injury and overwork, the horses had to endure explosions, bright flashes of light from bursting shells and the smell of blood – all things that were terrifying to them.

Huge numbers of horses died during the conflict – more horses than men were killed at the infamous battles of the Somme and Passchendaele.

GRAMMAR, PUNCTUATION & SPELLING ▼

1. Modal verbs

Objective

To use modal verbs or adverbs to indicate degrees of possibility.

What you need

Interactive activity 'Modal verbs', photocopiable page 22 'How likely is that?'.

What to do

- Introduce the children to modal verbs by explaining that they are words we use to indicate likelihood, permission, ability or obligation; to show if we believe something is certain, probable or possible.

- Display the following pairs of words that you have already written on the board: 'may' – 'might'; 'shall' – 'should'; 'will' – 'would'; 'must' – 'ought'; 'can' – 'could'. Explain that these are the most common modal verbs. Ask for examples of sentences containing any of them, for example, 'he may be able to go' or 'you must do your homework'.

- Display the interactive activity 'Modal verbs' and work through it with the children. If they are unsure which modal verb to choose, read each sentence three times, selecting each choice of word to determine the best fit.

- Hand out photocopiable page 22 'How likely is that?'. Explain that in the second part of this activity, modal adverbs are used to serve a similar purpose to modal verbs – to indicate degrees of possibility. In this case, they are invited to compose their own sentences using modal adverbs. Ask the children to complete the activity independently.

Differentiation

Support: Allow the children to complete only the first section of the activity.

2. Creating cohesion

Objective

To use devices to build cohesion within a paragraph.

What you need

Photocopiable page 23 'Make it flow'.

What to do

- Write the word 'cohesion' on the board, explaining that it means to bind things together to enable continuity. Explain that we use cohesion in writing to link together facts or events.

- Display these words that you have written previously: 'then', 'after that', 'this', 'firstly', 'however', 'even though'. Explain that these are used to create cohesion between sentences in a paragraph. Can the children think of others? (For example, 'as a result', 'subsequently', 'meanwhile', 'later'.)

- Give this example to demonstrate the use of cohesion: 'Many horses were requisitioned for the war. Subsequently, there were fewer animals to work at home.'

- Hand out photocopiable page 23 'Make it flow'. Read the passage aloud up to 'his call', omitting the spaces where the cohesive words will go. Invite the children to share their observations, agreeing that it sounds stilted. Ask them to complete the activity independently, choosing words to make the passage flow more smoothly. Each word is used once.

- When they have completed the task, invite the children to compare their choices with a partner. Did they make the same selections? Would they change any of their choices?

Differentiation

Support: Allow the children to work in pairs to complete the activity.
Extension: Challenge the children to write their own passage, with a follow-up paragraph about Joey's life, making use of appropriate cohesive words and phrases.

3. Parentheses

Objective

To use brackets, dashes or commas to indicate parenthesis.

What you need

Interactive activity 'Parentheses', photocopiable page 24 'Oh, by the way'.

What to do

- Introduce the children to the word 'parenthesis' and its plural 'parentheses'. Explain that they are brief interruptions in a sentence, acting as a kind of aside to the reader, giving further information or clarification. We always use brackets, dashes and commas in pairs before and after the interruption to form parentheses.

- On the board write: 'The farmers, who needed their horses, had to sell them to the army.' Draw attention to the placing of both commas and demonstrate that the sentence still makes sense when the parenthesis is removed.

- Display interactive activity 'Parentheses', working through each screen with the children and showing the use of each type of parenthesis. Ask the children to explain the reasons for their choices, talking through the correct answers.

- Hand out photocopiable page 24 'Oh, by the way' for the children to complete independently.

Differentiation

Support: Allow the children to complete the activity in pairs.
Extension: Challenge the children to write their own sentences about *War Horse*, using each type of parenthesis.

4. Punctuating lists

Objective

To use a colon to introduce a list and use semi-colons within lists.

What you need

Printable page 'Punctuating lists'.

Cross-curricular link

History

What to do

- Ensure the children are familiar with the colon, semi-colon and comma, and that they are used in general writing as indicators of pauses. Explain that we also use them when writing lists within another piece of writing. Colons indicate the start of the list; semi-colons are only used if the list items already contain commas.

- On the board write: 'A horse needs: fresh, clean hay; plentiful, cold water; careful, daily grooming; a place to shelter.' Point out the punctuation, demonstrating how the colon and semi-colon have been used to separate the different list items. Note that the commas are used to separate descriptive adjectives.

- Hand out printable page 'Punctuating lists' for the children to complete independently. Advise them to read through each sentence before they begin rewriting, to get an indication of how the list items are separated. They may pencil in the punctuation if they wish, checking their ideas before rewriting the correctly punctuated sentence.

Differentiation

Support: Show the children where the commas would go in the sentences, leaving them to insert the colons and semi-colons.
Extension: Invite the children to write their own correctly punctuated lists on a subject of their choice.

5. 'Able'/'ably' and 'ible'/'ibly'

Objective

To spell words ending in 'able', 'ible', 'ably' and 'ibly'.

What you need

Individual whiteboards and pens, printable page 'Make your choice', scissors, dictionaries interactive activity 'Which ending?'.

What to do

- On the board write: 'acceptable acceptible'. Invite the children to write the correct spelling on their individual whiteboards and show you their choices. Delete the incorrect spelling and repeat with other pairs of 'able'/'ible' words, such as 'serviceable', 'notable', 'horrible'. Continue with 'ably'/'ibly' endings, such as 'terribly', 'sizeably'.

- Explain that most words ending with 'able'/'ably' have a recognisable English root word, such as 'reason' – 'reasonable', whereas most words ending in 'ible'/'ibly' do not, such as 'illegible' (though there are exceptions, such as 'convertible'). Words ending in a hard 'g' or 'c' are always followed by 'able', for example 'navigable', 'amicable'.

- Hand out printable page 'Make your choice'. Invite the children to cut out the words and sort them into two lists – words they think they would find easier to learn to spell and those they would find trickier. Reassure them that everyone's lists will be different. Suggest they put unfamiliar words at the top of each list and use a dictionary to check their meanings.

- Ask the children to write the trickier words in their spelling journals, challenging themselves to learn them and their meanings.

- Invite them to complete interactive activity 'Which ending?' independently to assess their learning.

Differentiation

Support: Allow the children to reinforce their knowledge by working on the easier words first.

6. 'Ough' words

Objective

To spell words containing the letter string 'ough'.

What you need

Interactive activity 'Though, through, thorough', individual whiteboards and pens, printable page 'What sound does 'ough' make?'.

What to do

- On the board, write 'tough, dough, cough, bough, rough'. Ask: *Which two words rhyme?* ('tough', 'rough') Invite volunteers to read the other words. Explain that there are many ways to pronounce the 'ough' letter string. Ask: *What sounds do they make in these words?* (uff, oh, off, ow)

- Write on the board 'though, through, thorough'. Invite volunteers to read the words. Explain that these three 'ough' words are often confused. Display interactive activity 'Though, through, thorough' and work through it with the children. For each sentence, ask them to write and show you the word they think is correct on their individual whiteboards before you select the most popular answer to see if they were correct. Alternatively, the children could do the activity independently.

- Hand out printable page 'What sound does 'ough' make?' for the children to complete independently.

Differentiation

Support: Suggest the children write the words they are confident in reading, allowing them to omit any they are not familiar with.
Extension: Encourage the children to create a display of 'ough' words similar to the boxes on the printable page, adding extra words they have thought of.

How likely is that?

● Modal verbs are used to indicate likelihood, ability, permission or obligation. Underline the modal verbs in these sentences. One is done for you.

1. Everyone thought there <u>might</u> be a war.

2. Albert knew he could teach Joey to be a farm horse.

3. 'I will join up to go to France with Joey,' said Albert.

4. Albert knew Joey could be killed or injured in the war.

5. Joey felt that he may be treated well by Emilie.

6. It seemed clear that Topthorn and Joey would become friends.

● We can also use modal adverbs in a similar way. Write your own sentences including your choice of these modal adverbs.

certainly	rarely	perhaps
possibly	definitely	clearly

_____

_____

_____

_____

_____

_____

_____

_____

Make it flow

● Choose words from the word bank. Write them in the spaces to make the paragraph flow smoothly so that it has cohesion.

then	after that	even though	afterwards	this
subsequently	however	at first	firstly	later

_____, Joey's life was untroubled. He knew nothing of what

lay in store. _____ everything changed. One dreadful day, Joey

was separated from his mother and taken to an auction where he was bought by a

drunken farmer.

_____ he found himself living on a different farm, expected to

work the land, _____ he had thoroughbred blood in his veins.

_____, it was here that Joey found the boy who was to be his

friend for life.

It fell to Albert to train Joey as a farm horse. _____, he lead Joey

over the fields, walking him up and down. _____, he began

lunging the horse and training him to come to his call. _____

came the difficult job of getting Joey used to wearing a collar so that

_____ he was able to pull a plough. _____

new skill would be one that he would use in years to come, but in very different

circumstances, and far from the farm he had come to call home.

Oh, by the way

- Brackets, dashes and commas are used when we give extra information in a sentence. This is called 'parenthesis' and is like a brief aside to the reader.
- Rewrite these sentences, putting in the parenthesis indicated.

1. Albert's father who got drunk every Tuesday treated Joey badly at first. (Add commas)

_____

_____

2. There was great celebration even though there was to be a war when the army arrived in town. (Add dashes)

_____

_____

3. Albert's mother sticking up for his father tried to explain why he was acting harshly towards Joey. (Add brackets)

_____

_____

4. Topthorn a stronger animal acted as Joey's friend and mentor. (Add commas)

_____

_____

5. His first battle even though he had been prepared was a terrifying experience for Joey. (Add dashes)

_____

_____

1. True friends

Objective

To summarise the main ideas drawn from more than one paragraph, identifying key details that support the main ideas.

What you need

Copies of *War Horse*, individual whiteboards and pens, sticky notes, two or three large sheets of sugar paper.

What to do

- Ensure the children are familiar with the first five chapters of the book before the lesson.

- Invite them to focus on the bond between Joey and Albert, which is established early in the book. Ask the children to skim read from 'I was left there with no water' in Chapter 1 to 'trotted up into the village' in Chapter 4. Working in pairs, invite them to note on individual whiteboards anything that shows us how this bond was forged.

- After 15–20 minutes, ask each pair to join another pair to share and discuss their observations. Hand out five or six sticky notes to each set of four children, asking them to choose their most interesting points, writing one on each of the sticky notes. They should then attach these to the large sheets of sugar paper, which you have pinned to a wall.

- When they have finished, group the notes that are similar together, discussing each idea with the class. Can they suggest how important it was to the whole story to have this close bond between Albert and Joey, when it is Joey's story we learn about rather than Albert's?

Differentiation

Support: Allow the children to read just the first two chapters.

2. Albert

Objective

To draw inferences such as inferring characters' feelings, thoughts and motives from their actions, and justifying with evidence.

What you need

Copies of *War Horse*, interactive activity 'What would Albert do?', photocopiable page 29 'Albert'.

Cross-curricular link

PSHE

What to do

- The children should be familiar with the first four chapters of the book before the lesson. Invite their opinions of Albert, asking for evidence to support their views.

- Together or independently, read Chapter 1 from 'I was left there' to the end. What words would they use to describe Albert here, and why? For example: 'gentle', 'admiring', 'enthusiastic', 'caring'.

- Repeat the task after reading Chapter 2, from 'That next morning' to 'long as he's sober'. Suggested words might include 'trainer', 'protector', 'stern'.

- Continue the task with Chapter 4, from 'I had just about' to the end of the chapter. They may suggest 'spirited', 'eager', 'keen', 'determined', 'brave'.

- Display interactive activity 'What would Albert do?', working through one screen at a time, discussing the children's choices and asking them to justify their selections.

- Hand out photocopiable page 29 'Albert' for the children to complete independently.

Differentiation

Support: Allow the children to select just two words to explain on the photocopiable sheet.
Extension: Encourage the children to provide justification for several more of their selected words on the back of the sheet.

3. The battlefield

Objective

To identify how language contributes to meaning.

What you need

Copies of *War Horse*, photocopiable page 30 'Words that make a difference'.

Cross-curricular link

History

What to do

- Read aloud, or ask the children to read to themselves, from the opening of Chapter 8 up to 'dead and dying'. Ask for their immediate reactions to the vivid description of the battlefield, discussing their observations.

- Talk together about how Michael Morpurgo has succeeded in creating atmosphere and ask the children how they think he achieved this. They may pick out vocabulary, the way he moves the action from quiet to noise and back to quiet again, or that he doesn't shy away from describing the horrors of war.

- Explain that this section is a good example of where the author has made deliberate vocabulary choices to create the desired effect. Ensure the children know about alliteration and assonance, giving the examples of 'heavy horses' and 'ran madly' to demonstrate.

- Hand out photocopiable page 30, 'Words that make a difference' for the children to complete in pairs, referring to their copies of the book.

- Draw the class together and invite the children to share some of their choices, explaining their reasons.

Differentiation

Support: Allow the children to work up to 'dead and dying' when completing the sheet.
Extension: Ask the children to work to the end of the chapter when completing the sheet.

4. Three owners

Objective

To summarise the main ideas drawn from more than one paragraph, identifying key details that support the main ideas.

What you need

Individual whiteboards and pens, printable page 'Three owners'.

Cross-curricular links

PSHE, drama

What to do

- Remind the children that throughout the book, Joey has several owners or carers. Ask them to think about Albert, Heinrich and Emilie. Invite their observations on how Joey felt when in the care of each of them, asking them to justify their answers.

- Give them ten minutes to think of questions they could ask each of the characters, noting them on individual whiteboards.

- Invite volunteers to sit in the hot seat, in role as one of the characters, for the other children to ask their questions, making sure each character is used.

- After the hot-seat activity, invite the children to suggest ways in which the characters are similar and how they are different. For example, they all cared well for Joey and he responded well to each of them; all were directly involved in the war; none of them felt war was a good thing; they were different nationalities and ages; two were soldiers, one just a child.

- Hand out printable page 'Three owners' for the children to complete independently.

Differentiation

Extension: Challenge the children to write a paragraph in role as one of the characters, talking about their time with Joey.

5. Horses and soldiers

Objective

To identify and discuss themes in and across a wide range of writing.

What you need

Media resource 'Horses in battle', media resource 'Western Front mud'.

Cross-curricular link

History

What to do

- Ask the children how they would summarise the story *War Horse*. What would they say it is about? Agree that it focuses on a horse's experiences during World War I.

- Display media resource 'Horses in battle' and ask for the children's reactions to this depiction of cavalry horses amid gunfire. Invite the children to express their opinions about the use of horses in battle.

- Display media resource 'Western Front mud', showing soldiers on the battlefield. Ask: *What are your thoughts about soldiers fighting in the war?* Allow them to express their opinions. Ask what similarities they can think of between the experiences of horses and men in the war, listing their suggestions on the board. (For example, all endured: front-line fighting, muddy and freezing conditions, rationed food, the sight of dead and injured men and horses, separation from family.)

- Ask: *Why might Michael Morpurgo have chosen to focus his story on a horse rather than a young soldier?* (For example, to depict war from a different perspective, to show that horses experienced similar conditions to soldiers, to make us aware that horses were used in the war.) Had the children realised before reading the book that horses played an important part in hostilities?

6. Time marches on

Objective

To identify how structure contributes to meaning.

What you need

Copy of *War Horse*, printable page 'Time passing'.

Cross-curricular link

History

What to do

- Read the opening sentences from Chapters 2, 3, 5, 11, 12, 14 and 18. Ask the children what they have in common, agreeing that they all show the passage of time in some way. Read each sentence again, identifying the time elements in each.

- Ask: *Why was it necessary for Michael Morpurgo to start the chapters this way?* (The story covers at least a six-year period and he needed to focus on the key events.) Explain that because Joey summarises the intervening time for us, we still have a good idea of what happened.

- Hand out printable page 'Time passing' for the children to complete independently. Explain that although they are asked to use events from the story, these don't necessarily have to fit the sentence openings given – if they cannot remember whether something happened after winter or spring, it doesn't matter for this exercise. When composing their own time-linked openings, they could refer to the seasons and use phrases such as 'much later', 'years had passed', and 'the following months flew by'.

Differentiation

Support: Allow the children to complete just the first task on the sheet.
Extension: Encourage the children to complete a partner's new sentence openings, referring to events in the story.

7. They meet again

Objective

To discuss and evaluate how authors use language, considering the impact on the reader.

What you need

Copies of *War Horse*, individual whiteboards and pens.

What to do

- To prepare for the lesson, ask the children to read Chapter 17 of *War Horse*. Alternatively, read it to them, from 'Yes, Sergeant' to the end of the chapter. Here we see Joey being reunited with Albert at the veterinary hospital.

- Point out that we know Albert and Joey have been reunited before Albert realises himself. Ask the children to work in pairs, looking through the chapter, noting on individual whiteboards the ways in which Michael Morpurgo has created tension and a sense of expectation for readers when boy and horse are reunited. For example, he lets us know who both characters are straight away but makes Albert wait; he lets us see Joey's frustration and impatience at trying to communicate with Albert; he makes another soldier the one who slowly uncovers Joey's distinctive markings; he uses dialogue rather than description to show us what is happening; he extends the final discovery rather than let them realise straight away.

- Invite the children to share and discuss their observations. Ask how reading this chapter made them feel. Ask: *How effective was Michael Morpurgo's writing in creating tension and a sense of expectation?*

Differentiation

Support: Allow the children to just read from 'The two men worked tirelessly on me'.

8. How Joey felt

Objective

To draw inferences, such as inferring characters' feelings, thoughts and motives from their actions, and justifying with evidence.

What you need

Copy of *War Horse*, photocopiable page 31 'How did Joey feel?'.

Cross-curricular link

PSHE

What to do

- Remind the children that *War Horse* is written in the first person, so we learn about events from Joey's point of view, as a horse. Read Chapter 2, from 'I must have been standing asleep' to 'turned on his heel to go', asking the children to listen out for when Joey's feelings are mentioned ('my heart thumping wildly with fear. Terrified, I knew I could not run' and 'I noticed with infinite pride and pleasure'). Given the content of the extract, we might have expected to learn more of Joey's reactions to what he heard and what happened. However, it is not difficult for us to imagine as we are able to put ourselves in Joey's position.

- Hand out photocopiable page 31 'How did Joey feel?', and go through the events listed as reminders, briefly discussing what happened in each one. Ask the children to complete the sheet independently. Invite them to share and discuss their responses afterwards with a partner.

Differentiation

Support: Allow the children to list just descriptive words or short phrases for each event.
Extension: Ask the children to write their response in sentences, using descriptive language.

Albert

- Circle adjectives in the box that could be used to describe an aspect of Albert's character.
- Select four of your words and explain your reasons for choosing them, referring to incidents in the first four chapters of the story.

kind	brave	argumentative	unsympathetic
determined	protective	uncaring	stubborn
lazy	gentle	eager	forgiving
reckless	firm	spirited	loyal

1. Word: _____

Explanation: _____

_____

_____

2. Word: _____

Explanation: _____

_____

_____

3. Word: _____

Explanation: _____

_____

_____

4. Word: _____

Explanation: _____

_____

_____

Words that make a difference

● Complete the boxes when you have identified examples of each word type in Chapter 8 of *War Horse*.

Words that describe what could be heard

Words that describe what could be seen

Examples of alliteration

Examples of assonance

Powerful verbs

How did Joey feel?

● We know the things that happened to Joey through his own words, but he doesn't tell us how he felt in his descriptions of events. How do you think he felt? Complete the grid below with your ideas.

Event	How I think Joey felt
When he was separated from his mother.	
When he met Albert and started to get to know him.	
When he was sold to the army.	
When he went into his first battle.	
When he was captured by the enemy.	
When he was trapped in the wire in no man's land.	
When he was reunited with Albert.	

TALK ABOUT IT

1. After the sale

What to do

- Read Chapter 4 of *War Horse*, where Joey is sold to the army. Ask the children to imagine the scene afterwards, when Albert and his parents are together back at the farm, perhaps at the table eating their evening meal. Invite them to spend a couple of minutes silently thinking about what each character would be experiencing. Then ask them to share their thoughts with a partner.

- Hand out photocopiable page 35 'After the sale' for them to complete independently, writing their ideas about what the characters might say to each other.

- When they are finished, organise the children into groups of three to role play the conversation between Albert and his father and mother, using their notes to guide them. They will need to decide which character would begin the conversation. Remind them that although they have given some thought to each character's state of mind, the way the conversation develops will also depend upon listening and reacting to each other, so new ideas will probably emerge.

- Invite volunteer groups to perform their improvisations to the class.

2. Points of view

What to do

- Display Extract 4 for the children to read as a reminder about horses being requisitioned for use in World War I. Suggest that there were three key groups with a vested interest in this process – the military, the horse owners and the horses. Although the horses could not, of course, speak for themselves, seeing events through Joey's eyes in *War Horse* enables us to have that new perspective. Display media resource 'Horses on the Somme' to contextualise the situation.

- Display interactive activity 'Points of view', working through it with the children, discussing each statement until you come to an agreement about which groups would be most likely to say them.

- Divide the class into three equal groups, chosen randomly, one to represent each of the groups on the interactive activity: military officials, horse owners and horses. Ask each group to discuss how they feel about horses being taken for war duties, encouraging everyone to participate.

- After five to ten minutes of discussion, rearrange the groups so that new groups are formed, consisting of military officials, horse owners and horses. These could be smaller groups of six to eight. Ask the children to continue in role, sharing their concerns and responding to opinions and observations.

- Draw the class back together, inviting representatives from each group to share key points of their in-role discussions.

3. Grandfather in the hot seat

Objective

To ask relevant questions to extend their understanding and knowledge.

What you need

Photocopiable page 36 'Grandfather in the hot seat'.

Cross-curricular links

History, drama

What to do

- Remind the children about the time Joey spent with Emilie and her grandfather (found in Chapters 10 and 11), and her grandfather's surprise reappearance at the end of the story. Ask: *How would you describe the character of Emilie's grandfather?* Discuss their responses.

- Explain that you are going to put her grandfather in the hot seat. Hand out photocopiable page 36 'Grandfather in the hot seat', inviting the children to plan questions to ask him about the various topics listed on the sheet. Remind them to start their questions with words such as 'why',' when', 'where', 'what', 'who' and 'how' to avoid simple yes/no replies. Allow them ten minutes to complete this.

- Invite volunteers to act as Emilie's grandfather, responding to the children's questions. Change volunteers several times.

Differentiation

Support: Allow the children to write just one question for each topic on the sheet.
Extension: Encourage the children to think of two or more questions for each topic.

4. In the trenches

Objective

To participate in role play and improvisation.

What you need

Media resource 'Trench', Media resource 'Horses crossing a trench', media resource 'Soldier reading a book'.

Cross-curricular links

History, drama

What to do

- Begin by asking the children what they know about conditions on the battlefields of World War I. Display media resource 'Trench', explaining that many miles of trenches were dug by both German and Allied troops during the course of the war. Can they work out why they were needed? (To keep troops hidden and safe.) Have they realised that soldiers would first have to dig and shore up the trenches before they could be used?

- Display media resource 'Horses crossing a trench', reminding them that both horses and men were involved. Discuss what conditions were like in the trenches, particularly in bad weather or during bombardment.

- Display media resource 'Soldier reading a book' to show that there were also times of calm amid the fighting.

- Working in groups of three to six, ask the children to plan and rehearse a short role play set in a trench during the war. They should decide on their roles, the time of day and year, and whether their scene will include a battle, a time of respite, or both. Will they include an officer? Will the weather affect their scene and what the characters say? Will the soldiers be experienced or new to battle?

- After planning and rehearsal, invite groups to perform their scenes to the rest of the class.

5. What do you think about the war?

Objective
To maintain attention and participate actively in collaborative conversations.

What you need
Media resource '1914 recruiting poster', media resource 'Horses in battle', photocopiable page 37 'Pros and cons'.

Cross-curricular link
History

What to do

- Display media resource '1914 recruiting poster', asking for the children's reactions and comments. Would it persuade them to enlist in the services at the outbreak of war? Remind them that the story *War Horse* is set during that war, showing us the truth of what awaited both soldiers and horses.

- Display media resource 'Horses in battle', again inviting their comments.

- Explain that to prepare for a discussion, they will have the opportunity to do some preparatory thinking. Hand out photocopiable page 37 'Pros and cons', explaining the meaning of the title (points in favour and points against). Allow the children to discuss their thinking with a partner, noting their key points for later reference.

- After 15 minutes, draw the class together and invite the children to share some of their notes for general discussion. Encourage all the children to participate, and stress active listening and polite debate. After the discussion, ask for a show of hands to see whether the class felt the war was a good or bad thing.

- If you wish to follow up this activity with a writing task, go to Get writing 'Should there have been a war?' (page 39).

6. Afterwards

Objective
To give well-structured descriptions, explanations and narratives for different purposes, including for expressing feelings.

What you need
Copy of *War Horse*, printable page 'Afterwards'.

Cross-curricular links
Drama, history

What to do

- Read the final two paragraphs of the book. Ask the children to think about what life might have been like for Joey and Albert after the war. Invite them to imagine what an older Albert might say about the events he experienced before and during the war.

- Arrange the children into groups of three or four, handing out one copy of printable page 'Afterwards' to each group. Ask them to appoint a scribe for the group. Invite the groups to go through the points on the sheet, discussing each one and choosing one or two for their scribe to write on the sheet. Encourage them to consider Albert's feelings as well as describing his experiences.

- After 15–20 minutes, go through the list, inviting the groups to share their thinking and extend to a whole-class discussion.

Differentiation

Extension: Invite volunteers to perform a monologue in role as Albert, using the notes and discussion as stimulus. Individuals could be chosen for each separate point on the printable page.

After the sale

● Imagine Albert and his parents are back at the farm after Joey has been sold to the army. What would each of them be thinking? Make notes about what they might say to each other.

Albert

Albert's father

Albert's mother

Grandfather in the hot seat

● To plan for putting Emilie's grandfather in the hot seat, write some of the questions you could ask him about each of the following.

1. His granddaughter, Emilie

2. Being invaded by the German Army

3. Joey

4. The horse auction, when he bought Joey back

5. His life before the war

6. Any other questions

Pros and cons

● From what you know, how do you feel about World War I? Note your thoughts below to prepare for a discussion.

Pros – why the war was a good thing	Cons – why the war was a bad thing

● In a sentence, sum up your feelings about the war.

_____

_____

GET WRITING

1. A horse's plea

Objective
To select appropriate grammar and vocabulary, understanding how such choices can change and enhance meaning.

What you need
Media resources 'Horses on the Somme', 'Horses in battle', 'Horses being fed', 'Horses dragging artillery', photocopiable page 41 'A horse's plea'.

Cross-curricular link
History

What to do
- Display media resources 'Horses on the Somme', 'Horses in battle', 'Horses being fed' and 'Horses dragging artillery'. After each one, discuss the conditions the horses were experiencing. Remind the children that the horses were requisitioned and trained to be part of the war, having no choice in the matter. Ask: *What do you think they would have thought about their experiences?* Discuss their comments.

- Hand out photocopiable page 41 'A horse's plea'. Explain that the children are going to write a non-rhyming poem in role as a horse during the war, titled 'A horse's plea'. Ensure they understand the word 'plea'. Invite them to complete the page as a planning sheet to gather ideas for their poem.

- When they have finished their planning, they can begin to write their poems. Encourage them to select their vocabulary carefully in order to evoke atmosphere, reminding them of Michael Morpurgo's deliberate word choices in the story.

Differentiation
Support: Suggest opening lines, such as 'Here I am…', which can be repeated for each stanza.
Extension: Challenge the children to write a second poem, from a soldier's point of view, entitled 'A soldier's plea'.

2. Trooper Warren's letter

Objective
To describe settings, characters and atmosphere in narratives and integrate dialogue to convey character and advance the action.

What you need
Copy of *War Horse*.

Cross-curricular links
History, PSHE

What to do
- Read the children the letter from Trooper Warren's mother in Chapter 7. Ask: *What does the letter tell us about Trooper Warren and his family?* For example, we know the family are farmers living in a village, that Trooper Warren's name is Charlie, that he has a younger brother, and a girlfriend called Sally. Ask: *What do you notice about the contents of the letter?* Agree that there is little news – nothing much seems to happen.

- Ask: *How would Trooper Warren feel to receive the letter?* Discuss their thoughts.

- Ask the children to spend a few minutes talking with a partner about how the trooper might reply to the letter. What might he write about? Would he be completely honest about what was happening around him in the war? What would he tell his family about Joey? To help their thinking, read to them again from Chapter 7, from 'It was during these long, stifling marches' to 'used effectively'.

- After ten minutes of planning time, ask the children to compose their replies to the letter, in role as Trooper Warren.

- For authenticity, allow the children to rewrite their letters on writing paper and place them in envelopes. Create a display together with the letter from his mother.

3. Should there have been a war?

Objective

To use further organisational and presentational devices to structure text and to guide the reader (for example, headings, bullet points, underlining).

What you need

Photocopiable page 37 'Pros and cons', individual whiteboards and pens.

Cross-curricular links

History, PSHE

What to do

- This writing activity can be used as a follow-up to Talk about it 'What do you think about the war?' (page 34). If doing this, refer the children to their completed photocopiable page 37 'Pros and cons'. If not, hand out the sheet and ask the children to discuss with a partner possible reasons for and against the war, keeping a note of their ideas on the sheet.

- After 10–15 minutes, draw the class together. Explain that they will be writing a non-fiction piece expressing the arguments for and against the war. You may wish to allow the children some time to do further research about the causes of World War I to provide extra information to support their arguments.

- When they are ready to begin writing, ask how they will organise their writing. What title will they have and what subheadings? Can they make use of bullet points for lists, or underlining for emphasis? Allow them to plan an outline of their piece on individual whiteboards before they write.

Differentiation

Support: Suggest the children limit themselves to two reasons for and two reasons against the war.
Extension: Encourage the children to discuss at least four reasons for and four reasons against the war.

4. Joey remembers

Objective

To describe settings, characters and atmosphere in narratives and integrate dialogue to convey character and advance the action.

What you need

Photocopiable page 42 'Joey remembers', individual whiteboards and pens.

Cross-curricular links

History, PSHE

What to do

- Remind the children that *War Horse* is written in the first person, from Joey's point of view as a horse. Through his words, we see his interactions with other characters. Invite the children to focus on four of these – Albert, Captain Nicholls, Topthorn and Friedrich.

- Hand out photocopiable page 42 'Joey remembers'. Invite the children to talk with a partner about things that Joey shared with each of the characters, perhaps noting these on individual whiteboards as they work. After ten minutes, ask them to complete the sheet independently.

- Invite the children to use their completed sheet to write four paragraphs, one for each character, describing in Joey's voice his memories of shared experiences with each one, and how he felt about them. Encourage them to use a wide and interesting vocabulary to describe settings and evoke atmosphere, and to use some dialogue to aid characterisation and give pace and interest to the narrative.

Differentiation

Support: Allow the children to choose two of the characters to write about.

5. Précis

Objective

To précis longer passages.

What you need

Interactive activity 'Practising précis', photocopiable page 43 'Précis practice', Extract 3.

Cross-curricular link

History

What to do

- On the board, write the word 'précis'. Ask: *Does anyone know this word?* Explain that it is a French word meaning 'specific' and is similar to the word 'precise'. We use it to mean 'summarise' or 'to sum up'. In writing, this is when we rewrite a piece using fewer words.

- Explain that when we précis we look for the key points. We may delete adjectives or adverbs, reword long phrases to shorten them, move words around and reword descriptions.

- Display interactive activity 'Practising précis', working through each screen with the children. For example, screen 1 might be shortened to 'During World War I, the army trained many requisitioned horses for use overseas.' Be prepared to try several versions before agreeing on the best summary of each sentence on the three screens.

- Hand out photocopiable page 43 'Précis practice' for the children to complete in pairs.

- Display Extract 3 and challenge the children to précis it on a sheet of paper or in their books.

Differentiation

Support: Allow the children to complete only the photocopiable sheet.

6. Officer's log

Objective

To describe settings, characters and atmosphere in narratives and integrate dialogue to convey character and advance the action.

What you need

Copy of *War Horse*, printable page 'Officer's log planning sheet'.

Cross-curricular links

History, computing

What to do

- The children should be familiar with Chapter 18 before the lesson. Begin by inviting them to say something about what went on in the veterinary hospital described in the chapter. Ask the children to imagine what a wartime veterinary hospital would have been like, inviting them to share their ideas. Encourage them to use their senses when giving their descriptions.

- Hand out printable page 'Officer's log planning sheet'. Invite them to put themselves in the position of an officer in charge of a wartime veterinary hospital and complete the planning sheet after discussing with a partner.

- When their planning is finished, they should use their sheets as a guide to write a daily log in role as the officer in charge. Remind them that they will be writing in the first person. To make their writing more interesting, encourage them to include the officer's feelings, hopes and fears as well as describing daily events. Suggest they include two or three other characters and snippets of conversation to enliven their writing.

Differentiation

Support: Suggest they focus on two or three elements of the officer's daily life, or his care for one particular horse.
Extension: Encourage them to develop the character of the officer through his voice.

A horse's plea

● What would a World War I military horse think about? What would it hope for? Consider the points below, making notes that you can use for your poem.

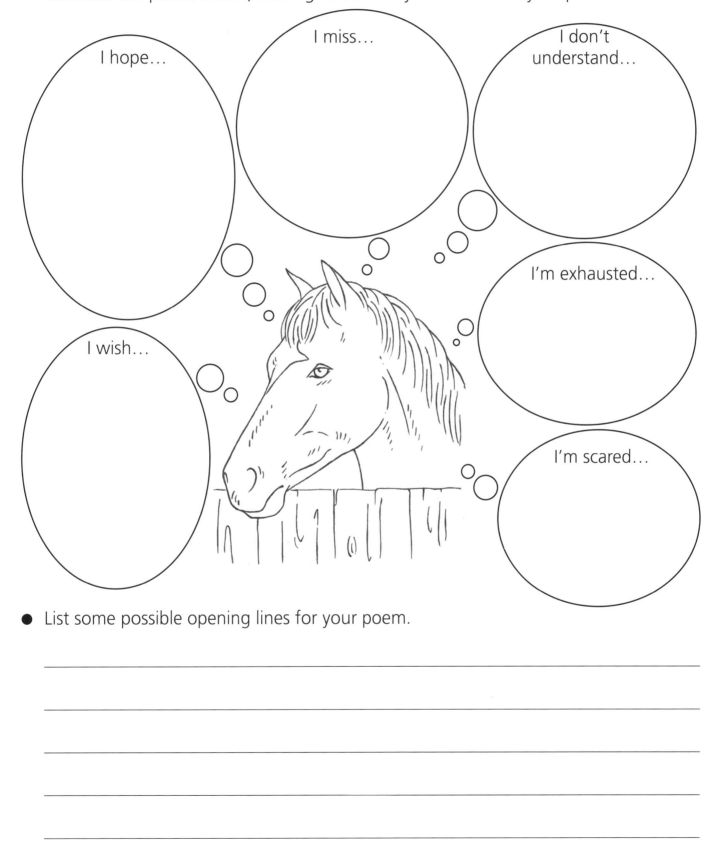

I hope…

I miss…

I don't understand…

I'm exhausted…

I wish…

I'm scared…

● List some possible opening lines for your poem.

_____

_____

_____

_____

_____

Joey remembers

● What would Joey remember about these key characters from his life? Write down what he would recall most, including how he felt as they came and went from his life.

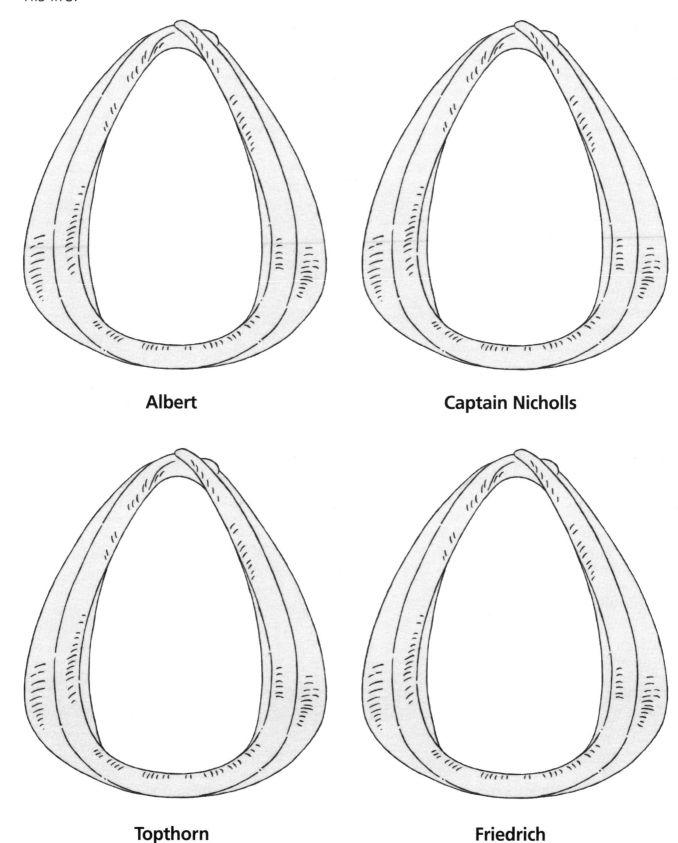

Albert

Captain Nicholls

Topthorn

Friedrich

Précis practice

● Write a précis of each paragraph.

In the early 20th century, horses were vital to the everyday life of everyone, whether they lived in the quiet countryside or a busy, bustling town. The practical tasks that are carried out today by enormous machines were mostly done by hard-working horses. Whatever the weather, on farms everywhere they were relied upon for ploughing, harrowing, harvesting; pulling hay, potatoes, wheat or muck; and many other heavy jobs that a tractor would do now.

_____

_____

_____

_____

_____

_____

In our towns and cities, horses could be seen on every street. They pulled heavy carts containing anything that needed moving. The familiar clip-clopping would herald the arrival of the milkman, coalman or rag-and-bone cart. Horses pulled early omnibuses – or buses for short – transporting people to their destinations. Imagine the effects of all these animals on the streets – not only were they noisy but the smells and mess they left behind we would probably find pretty difficult to cope with!

_____

_____

_____

_____

_____

_____

▼ ASSESSMENT

1. A recommendation

Objective
To recommend books that they have read to their peers, giving reasons for their choices.

What you need
Any reviews of books for children (either paper- or web-based), copies of *War Horse*.

What to do

- Ask the children how they choose new books to read. Do any of them use reviews? Read out some book reviews that you have sourced. Ask: *Would any of the reviews persuade you to try out the books?*

- Invite them to consider what they would tell other children about *War Horse*, explaining why they would or would not recommend it. Ask them to make some notes about, for example, what they would say about: the key events and the main characters; the quality of the writing; who might enjoy the book; how they would sum up the book overall. Explain that they should give reasons for their opinions. They may refer to a copy of the book while they do this to act as a reminder.

- After 10–15 minutes, ask them to write their review or recommendation of the book.

- Well-considered recommendations will cover a wide range of well-supported points, giving a clear idea of the child's thoughts about the book.

Differentiation
Support: Allow the children to submit their review or recommendation under the headings suggested.
Extension: Encourage the children to refer to specific incidents or take quotes from the book to illustrate their points.

2. Joey's role on the wall

Objective
To describe settings, characters and atmosphere in narratives and integrate dialogue to convey character and advance the action.

What you need
Photocopiable page 47 'Joey's role on the wall'.

What to do

- Invite the children to consider Joey. Remind them that the story is told through his words, including dialogue that he overhears. Because of this, we know from spoken descriptions what he looked like. Ask if they remember the description of the unveiling of Joey's distinctive markings when he arrived at the veterinary hospital covered in mud.

- Hand out photocopiable page 47 'Joey's role on the wall', asking the children to complete it as preparation for writing a description of Joey. On the sheet, they are asked to consider a physical description of Joey as well as their interpretation of his personality and character, which should include reference to how he reacts to what happens to him, his experiences, and how he deals with challenges and changes of ownership. Remind them to think about what happened to him before, during and after the war.

- They should use these as prompts for writing their description of Joey in paragraphs. Good descriptions will be detailed, include several events in Joey's life and accurately sum up his character with specific reference to supporting facts.

Differentiation
Support: Allow the children to just complete the photocopiable sheet.
Extension: Encourage the children to refer to specific incidents to support their descriptions, explaining why their chosen examples tell us particular things about Joey's personality and character.

3. Spellcheck

Objective

To spell words ending with 'able', 'ible', 'ably' and 'ibly'.

What you need

Printable page 'Spellcheck'.

Cross-curricular link

French

What to do

- On the board, write 'collaps_____', inviting the children to provide the ending of either 'able' or 'ible' to make the spelling correct (collapsible). Repeat with 'insuffer_____' (insufferable) and 'ed_____' (edible). The children may be interested to know that most of our words with these endings have come from French and are the same in that language, but with a different pronunciation.

- Continue, but this time asking for either 'ably' or 'ibly' endings. On the board, write 'prefer_____' (preferably) and 'incred_____' (incredibly).

- Hand out printable page 'Spellcheck' for the children to complete independently, to check how well they have learned the endings being assessed.

4. Modal check-up

Objective

To use modal verbs or adverbs to indicate degrees of possibility.

What you need

Printable page 'Modal check-up'.

What to do

- On the board write 'might' and 'must'. Ask: *What is the difference in meaning between the words?* Agree that 'might' indicates it is not definite, while 'must' is imperative. Remind the children about the use of modal verbs to indicate degrees of possibility.

- Continue by writing 'possibly' and 'probably' to demonstrate degrees of likelihood when using modal adverbs.

- Hand out printable page 'Modal check-up' for the children to complete independently.

- Correctly completed sheets will have identified all the modal verbs and adverbs and used them appropriately in well-constructed sentences.

Differentiation

Support: Allow the children to write two rather than four sentences.
Extension: Challenge the children to write sentences for all the identified modal verbs and adverbs, continuing on the back of the sheet.

5. *War Horse* quiz

Objective

To ask questions to improve their understanding.

What you need

Copies of *War Horse*.

What to do

- Ask the children if they watch TV quiz shows. Discuss their responses. Explain that some quizzes require contestants to give the answer with no prompting, whereas others offer multiple choices. Which do the children prefer? Do they find that multiple choices can sometimes be confusing?

- Explain that you would like the children to compile their own quiz based on *War Horse*. They should include both types of questions and, as compilers, they also need to provide the answers. Explain that with multiple-choice questions, suggested answers must have some likelihood of being correct. Suggest they offer three alternatives.

- Discuss how they might devise their questions. For example, they could be about characters or events, they could be one-word answers or require longer explanations. Work through three or four examples together. Suggest a question about Joey near the start of the book or one about Albert near the end. Perhaps ask a question about Joey's early training.

- Ask the children to compile their quizzes independently. When all are completed, with answers provided, invite volunteers to ask some of their questions to the class.

- Well-planned quizzes will cover a range of events and characters, with several in-depth questions and correct answers.

Differentiation

Support: Allow the children to provide five or more questions.
Extension: Encourage the children to provide at least eight questions.

6. Battle

Objective

To describe settings, characters and atmosphere in narratives and integrate dialogue to convey character and advance the action.

What you need

Copy of *War Horse*, media resource 'Horses in battle'.

Cross-curricular link

History

What to do

- Read Chapter 8 of *War Horse* to the children, up to 'dead and dying', where a battle in the war is described. Then read the penultimate paragraph in Chapter 14 for a further description. Invite the children's responses and draw attention to the use of the senses in the descriptions, focusing on sights and sounds. Note also the use of alliteration in the first extract.

- Display the media resource 'Horses in battle' and ask the children to plan and write their own description of a battle based on what they have read in the book and any other research they may have done. They may choose to write in the first or third person. Invite them to use their senses and to include some alliteration, as in the first extract. Encourage them to aim for a vivid atmosphere through their descriptions. They may wish to include some dialogue. They should write in paragraphs.

- In assessing the finished pieces, look for deliberate vocabulary choices that enhance their writing, mention of both sights and sounds of battle and a sense of atmosphere.

Joey's role on the wall

● To prepare for writing a description of Joey, fill in your observations and ideas in the role on the wall template below.

● Outside the drawing, write what he looks like. Inside the drawing, write about Joey's personality and character.

SCHOLASTIC

Available in this series:

978-1407-16066-5

978-1407-16053-5

978-1407-16054-2

978-1407-16055-9

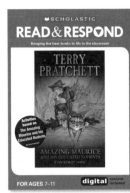

978-1407-16056-6

978-1407-16057-3

978-1407-16058-0

978-1407-16059-7

978-1407-16060-3

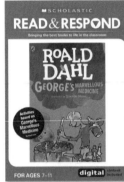

978-1407-16061-0

978-1407-16062-7

978-1407-16063-4

978-1407-16064-1

978-1407-16065-8 **JAN 2017**

978-1407-16052-8 **JAN 201**

978-1407-16067-2 **JAN 2017**

978-1407-16068-9 **JAN 2017**

978-1407-16069-6 **JAN 2017**

978-1407-16070-2 **JAN 2017**

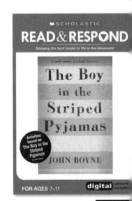

978-1407-16071-9 **JAN 20**

To find out more, call: 0845 6039091
or visit our website www.scholastic.co.uk/readandrespond